Birdwatcher's
GUIDE TO DELMARVA

Edited By: Curtis Badger
Photo By: Curtis Badger
Photo Manipulation By: Jerry Gerlitzki

acknowledgments

Special thanks to: Worcester County Department of Tourism and the Salisbury Zoological Park for raising the funds and organizing this guide from an idea into reality; the Coalition members for compiling the information; Curtis J. Badger for writing and editing the copy and providing several great photographs; Jerry Gerlitzki for the production and design of the guide; and the Delaware Department of Natural Resources and Environmental Control for offering the use of their CD library of photographs. Special recognition is given to the following organizations which offered major funding to make this guide possible:
Maryland Coastal Bays Program
Maryland Tourism Development Board
National Environmental Education and Training Foundation
National Fish and Wildlife Foundation, using federal matching funds provided by the U.S. National Fish and Wildlife Service
National Park Service
Rural Development Center, University of Maryland Eastern Shore, through a grant from the Economic Development Administration, U.S. Department of Commerce
Virginia Environmental Endowment

This publication is a project of the Delmarva Advisory Council's Atlantic Flyway Byway Consortium. The Consortium was formed as a tri-state effort to focus attention and give perspective to one of the greatest patterns of bird migration in the United States. For additional information, contact Delmarva Advisory Council, P.O. Box 4277, Salisbury, MD 21803-4277. • Phone 410/742-9271.

Printing Coordination: Panorama International Productions, Inc. dba Sierra Press
Sales & Distribution: Sierra Press
4988 Gold Leaf Drive
Mariposa, CA 95338
(800)-745-2631
Website: nationalparksusa.com
e-mail: siepress@yosemite.net

Printed in the Republic of South Korea.

First Printing 1999 -21M

contents

Photo By: Gary Mathie

birding on delmarva

Photo By: Curtis Badger

When most people think of birding on Delmarva, they envision ducks, geese, and long-legged wading birds such as herons and egrets. That's understandable. Most of the natural areas on Delmarva are home to waterfowl and wading birds. Visit Bombay Hook, Blackwater, or Chincoteague National Wildlife Refuges, and you leave with vivid impressions of snow geese, Canada geese, and great blue herons.

But the bird life of Delmarva is much more varied than that, ranging from waterfowl to colorful woodland warblers that have a decidedly tropical look. The checklist published by Chincoteague National Wildlife Refuge, alone, names more than 300 species that may be spotted there.

At Chincoteague, Blackwater, and Bombay Hook, waterfowl and wading birds are easy to see; you don't have to leave the comfort of your car. But please park that car, put on your walking shoes, and get out in the woods, especially in spring and fall when the songbird migration is at its peak. Only then will you appreciate the remarkable diversity of bird life on the Delmarva Peninsula.

While wildlife refuges on the coast were built with waterfowl in mind, most of them support a healthy songbird population, and natural resource managers have made it easy to see them by building hiking paths through wooded areas and thickets where the birds congregate. Assateague Island, Kiptopeke, Bombay Hook, Pocomoke River State Park, Pickering Creek, and many other sanctuaries on Delmarva are excellent places to see migrating songbirds, and the trails make viewing easy. Bring your binoculars and field guides, and learn about an exciting aspect of bird life on Delmarva.

the seasons of birds

The Delmarva Peninsula is used by many species of migrating birds. Ducks and geese arrive in the fall and will spend the winter here unless a hard freeze drives them farther south. Shorebirds move northward in great numbers in spring, and then return south in late summer. Songbirds pass through in spring and fall.

So, for Canada geese and warblers and hummingbirds, and for everything in between, Delmarva is nature's own interstate highway, complete with rest stops and restaurants.

For those of us interested in birds, there are no off-seasons on the coast. In the earliest months of the year there will be ducks and geese on the impoundments at the wildlife refuges. The inshore ocean waters will have thousands of sea ducks and pelagic birds such as northern gannets. At the Chesapeake Bay Bridge-Tunnel, the rock islands will be surrounded by scoters, oldsquaws, red-breasted mergansers, cormorants, and eiders. Great flocks of gulls will congregate, and uncommon species may be seen.

In spring, the shorebirds will move through. A favorite activity is to ride the back roads after a heavy rain and scan the farm fields with a spotting scope. There will be black-bellied plovers, sandpipers, yellowlegs, and many other species. Where there is standing water, there often will be dabbling ducks as well.

In April and May, the songbird and shorebird migration is at its peak. Barrier island beaches will get their annual visits from terns, skimmers, brown pelicans, and piping plovers - all of which will nest here. Gulls and rails will nest in the upper marshes and herons, egrets, and glossy ibis will congregate in noisy colonies in wooded hammocks on the marsh. Ospreys will nest in pine snags, on channel markers, or on special platforms constructed for them.

By the time the nesting season is waning, the shorebirds will move back through, with the greatest numbers occurring in late July and August. Any shallow waterway with tidal flats is a good place to see them.

In September, the peak movement of neotropical songbirds begins as they leave their nesting areas in the north and head south along well-used routes. The early migration will feature a wide variety of birds -- American redstarts, vireos, common yellowthroats, yellow warblers, Connecticut warblers, and many more. Later, by the end of October, there will be tens of thousands of yellow-rumped warblers, most of which will spend the winter.

Not coincidentally, the fall arrival of songbirds is accompanied by great flights of hawks. Kestrels will suddenly show up on fences and power lines, northern harriers will patrol the salt meadows, and the thickets and forests will be hunted by Cooper's and sharp-shinned hawks, the major predators of songbirds. Peregrine falcons and merlins will pass overhead as they follow the barrier island chain southward. Suddenly, the laughing gulls will be gone and ring-billed gulls will take their place.

This ever-changing kaleidoscope of bird life adds color and drama to the neighborhood, to the resident populations of wrens, cardinals, towhees, chickadees, nuthatches, blue jays, titmice and all the other birds one may consider standard fare. The intriguing thing about Delmarva is that, when you get out on the water or in the woods and salt marshes, you never know what birds you're likely to see.

☐ Red-necked Phalarop
☐ Red Phalarope

JAEGERS-GULLS-TE
☐ Pomarine Jaeger
☐ Parasitic Jaeger
☐ Laughing Gull*
☐ Franklin's Gull
☐ Little Gull
☐ Black-headed Gull
☐ Bonaparte's Gull
☐ Ring-billed Gull
☐ Herring Gull*
☐ Iceland Gull
☐ Lesser Black-backed
☐ Glaucous Gull
☐ Great Black-backed G
☐ Black-legged Kitiwak
☐ Gull-billed Tern*
☐ Caspian Tern*
☐ Royal Tern*
☐ Sandwich Tern*
☐ Roseate Tern
☐ Common Tern*
☐ Arctic Tern
☐ Forster's Tern*
☐ Least Tern*
☐ Bridled Tern
☐ Sooty Tern
☐ Black Tern
☐ Black Skimmer*
☐ Dovekie
☐ Thick-billed Murre
☐ Razorbill
☐ Atlantic Puffin

DOVES-CUCKOOS-C
☐ Rock Dove*
☐ Mourning Dove*
☐ Black-billed Cuckoo
☐ Yellow-billed Cuckoo
☐ Barn Owl*
☐ Eastern Screech-Owl
☐ Great Horned Owl*
☐ Snowy Owl
☐ Barred Owl*
☐ Long-eared Owl
☐ Short-eared Owl
☐ Northern Saw-whet C

**GOATSUCKERS-HUI
BIRDS-WOODPECKE**
☐ Common Nighthawk*
☐ Chuck-will's-widow*
☐ Whip-poor-will*
☐ Chimney Swift*
☐ Ruby-throated Humn
☐ Belted Kingfisher*
☐ Red-headed Woodpe
☐ Red-bellied Woodpec
☐ Yellow-bellied Sapsu
☐ Downy Woodpecker*
☐ Hairy Woodpecker*
☐ Northern Flicker*
☐ Pileated Woodpecker

FLYCATCHERS-SHRIK
☐ Olive-sided Flycatche
☐ Eastern Wood-Pewee
☐ Yellow-bellied Flycatc
☐ Acadian Flycatcher*
☐ Alder Flycatcher
☐ Willow Flycatcher
☐ Least Flycatcher
☐ Eastern Phoebe*

Delmarva events

APRIL
Ward World Championship Wildfowl Carving Competition, Ocean City, MD. This competition, held the last weekend in April, is the largest competition of wildfowl sculpture in the world. Entry levels from novice to world champion. Exhibiting artists with paintings and carvings. Friday, 10am-6pm; Saturday, 10am-8pm; Sunday, 10am-4pm. (410) 742-4988 Ext. 106.

Delmarva Birding Weekend, Birds of The World Photo Contest, Lower Eastern Shore, MD. The Delmarva Birding Weekend celebrates the migration of hundreds of warblers, shorebirds and waterfowl as well as many nesting birds and raptors. The weekend combines boat trips, canoe treks and expeditions by foot. Locations vary from the coastal bays of Assateague Island to the Pocomoke River to the Chesapeake Bay. Reservations required. Call for brochure, (800) 852-0335. skipjack.net/le_shore/visitworcester

MAY
International Migratory Bird Celebration, Eastern Shore of VA. This special event held at Chincoteague NWR and Eastern Shore of VA NWR to celebrate migratory birds is held annually on the second week in May. A variety of family activities from building birdhouses to creating crafty critters as well as various workshops and guided walks provide an enjoyable time for birders of all ages. For a schedule of activities or to make reservations for tours, contact Chincoteague NWR at (757) 336-6122 or Eastern Shore of Virginia NWR at (757) 331-2760.

Birding Festival, Smyrna, DE. This event, held in May, takes place at Bombay Hook and Prime Hook National Wildlife Refuges. Refuge tours as well as tours to other birding sites, nature walks, talks, canoe trips, crafts, games and live animal demonstrations are offered. (302) 653-6872.

JUNE- AUGUST
Guided Canoe Trips, Kiptopeke State Park, VA. Join us for guided canoe trips on beautiful Raccoon Creek. Canoe, gear and guide provided. The trips focus on the wildlife and ecology of the salt marsh. Inquire about our "Twilight" canoe trips held on each full moon. Every other week in season, once/month in the fall. Reservations required. (757) 331-2267.

Assateague Canoe Programs, Assateague State Park and Assateague Island National Seashore, MD. Each week canoe programs for both experienced and novice canoers are offered. The program themes are birdwatching and bay adventures. Reservations required. (410) 641-2120 (State Park), (410) 641-1441 (National Seashore).

SEPTEMBER-NOVEMBER
Fall Bird Banding and Hawk Observation Tours, Kiptopeke State Park, VA. From mid-September to mid-November, join the Park staff every Saturday morning for bird banding station tours and the hawk observatory tour. The bird banding tours include a brief orientation to birding, a short hike and visit to the banding station. The hawk observatory tour includes a visit to the hawk observatory to view hawk migration. Bring your binoculars!

OCTOBER
Eastern Shore Birding Festival, Lower Eastern Shore, VA. Perch at the hawk observatory and watch for peregrine falcons and merlins, with lots of songbirds too. Canoe trips, marsh and sand dune habitats, banding demonstrations and nearby Fisherman Island, Eastern Shore of Virginia NWR, Chincoteague NWR and Kiptopeke State Park make for an exciting weekend. Call for brochure. (757) 787-2460.

National Wildlife Refuge Week. The diversity of wild places and wildlife found on the more than 500 National Wildlife Refuges is celebrated during the second weekend of October at all Delmarva Wildlife Refuges. A variety of family activities, workshops and guided walks are provided. For more information, contact the National Wildlife Refuge you would like to visit.

Fisherman Island National Wildlife Refuge Tours, Eastern Shore of Virginia NWR. Fisherman Island is a haven for migrating raptors and songbirds. Wintering waterfowl use the island ponds and rafts of ducks are often spotted in the Chesapeake Bay. Tours are conducted on Saturdays through the middle of March. Guided hikes are 4-5 miles on soft and hard packed sand and take about 3 1/2 hours. Reservations required for tours. (757) 331-2760.

NOVEMBER
Waterfowl Festival, Easton, MD. Annual wildlife art show and sale held each year in mid-November. 450 artists display paintings, carvings, sculptures, decoys and gifts throughout historic downtown Easton. Admission. (410) 822-4567.

Waterfowl Week, Chincoteague, VA. From the Saturday before Thanksgiving to the Sunday after Thanksgiving, Chincoteague National Wildlife Refuge celebrates the marvel of migration. Special access will be offered on the Wildlife Loop and Service Road beginning Thanksgiving day through Sunday from noon to 3:30 pm. The Wildlife Loop opens from 9:00 am to dusk for the entire nine days to view wintering Canada and snow geese, swans and ducks. Guided walks and auditorium programs will also be offered. (757) 336-6122.

DECEMBER
Christmas Bird Counts. Held the week before Christmas to the week after Christmas, Christmas Bird Counts allows beginners to bird with more experienced people, allows an opportunity to volunteer for count organizers and it provides valuable data about wintering bird populations. The following is a list of bird counts on Delmarva by state:

Delaware
Bombay Hook   Rehoboth Bay
Cape Henlopen-Prime Hook   Middletown
Contact the Delmarva Ornithological Society- c/o Backyard Bird Company, (302) 478-8300
Seaford-Nanticoke
Contact the Sussex Bird Club- Bill Fintell, (800) 788-6428.

Maryland
Numerous Christmas Counts take place on Maryland's Eastern Shore. For a complete listing, including contacts and phone numbers, checkout the Maryland Ornithological Society web site: www.mdbirds.org or call their voice mail: (800) 823-0050

Virginia
Christmas Bird Counts are held at Wachapreague, Chincoteague and Cape Charles.
Contact Chincoteague NWR (757) 336-6122 and Eastern Shore of Virginia NWR (757) 331-2760.

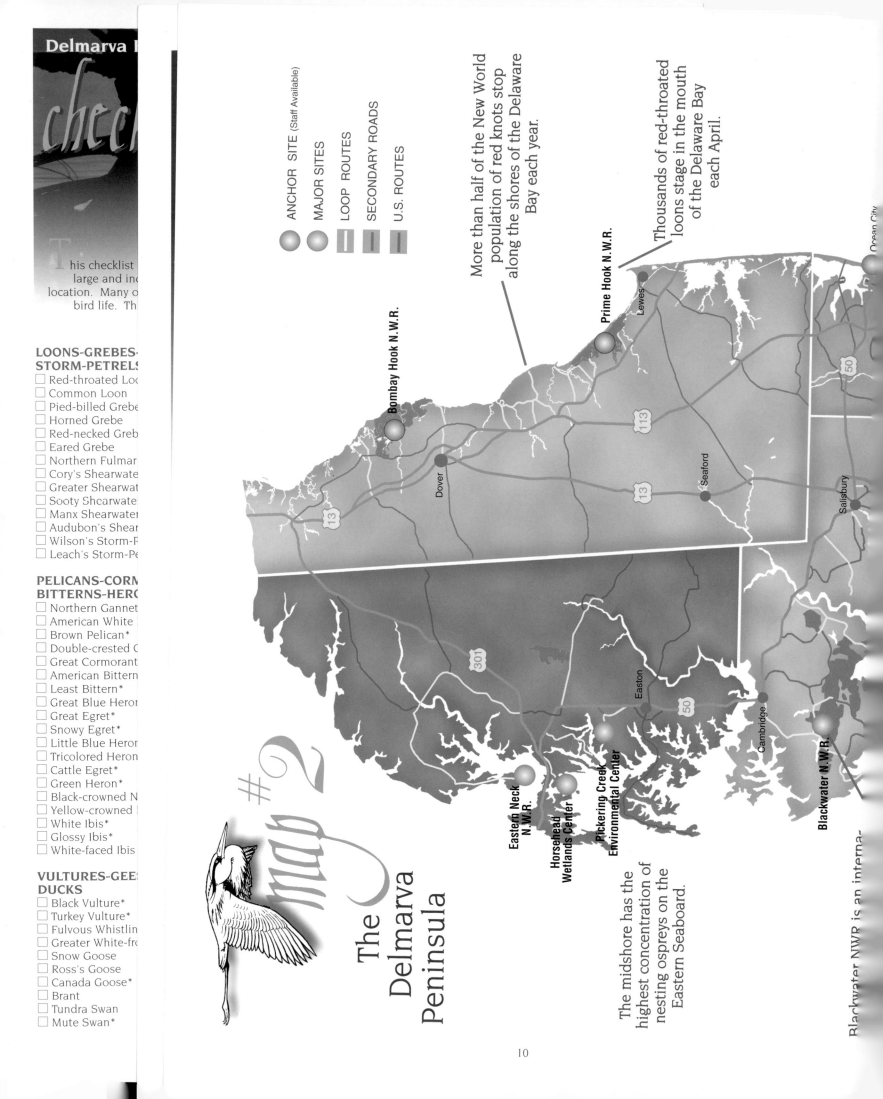

Delmarva (checklist header, partially visible)

This checklist [...]
large and in[...]
location. Many o[...]
bird life. Th[...]

**LOONS-GREBES-[...]
STORM-PETRELS[...]**

- [ ] Red-throated Loo[...]
- [ ] Common Loon
- [ ] Pied-billed Grebe[...]
- [ ] Horned Grebe
- [ ] Red-necked Greb[...]
- [ ] Eared Grebe
- [ ] Northern Fulmar[...]
- [ ] Cory's Shearwater[...]
- [ ] Greater Shearwat[...]
- [ ] Sooty Shearwate[...]
- [ ] Manx Shearwater[...]
- [ ] Audubon's Shear[...]
- [ ] Wilson's Storm-P[...]
- [ ] Leach's Storm-Pe[...]

**PELICANS-CORM[...]
BITTERNS-HERO[...]**

- [ ] Northern Gannet[...]
- [ ] American White [...]
- [ ] Brown Pelican*
- [ ] Double-crested C[...]
- [ ] Great Cormorant[...]
- [ ] American Bittern[...]
- [ ] Least Bittern*
- [ ] Great Blue Hero[...]
- [ ] Great Egret*
- [ ] Snowy Egret*
- [ ] Little Blue Heron[...]
- [ ] Tricolored Heron[...]
- [ ] Cattle Egret*
- [ ] Green Heron*
- [ ] Black-crowned N[...]
- [ ] Yellow-crowned [...]
- [ ] White Ibis*
- [ ] Glossy Ibis*
- [ ] White-faced Ibis[...]

**VULTURES-GEES[...]
DUCKS**

- [ ] Black Vulture*
- [ ] Turkey Vulture*
- [ ] Fulvous Whistlin[...]
- [ ] Greater White-fro[...]
- [ ] Snow Goose
- [ ] Ross's Goose
- [ ] Canada Goose*
- [ ] Brant
- [ ] Tundra Swan
- [ ] Mute Swan*

ANCHOR SITE (Staff Available)
MAJOR SITES
LOOP ROUTES
SECONDARY ROADS
U.S. ROUTES

More than half of the New World population of red knots stop along the shores of the Delaware Bay each year.

Thousands of red-throated loons stage in the mouth of the Delaware Bay each April.

Bombay Hook N.W.R.

Prime Hook N.W.R.

Lewes

113

13

Dover

Seaford

Salisbury

Ocean City

50

301

Easton

50

Cambridge

Blackwater N.W.R.

Eastern Neck N.W.R.

Horsehead Wetlands Center

Pickering Creek Environmental Center

map #2
The Delmarva Peninsula

The midshore has the highest concentration of nesting ospreys on the Eastern Seaboard.

Blackwater NWR is an interna[...]

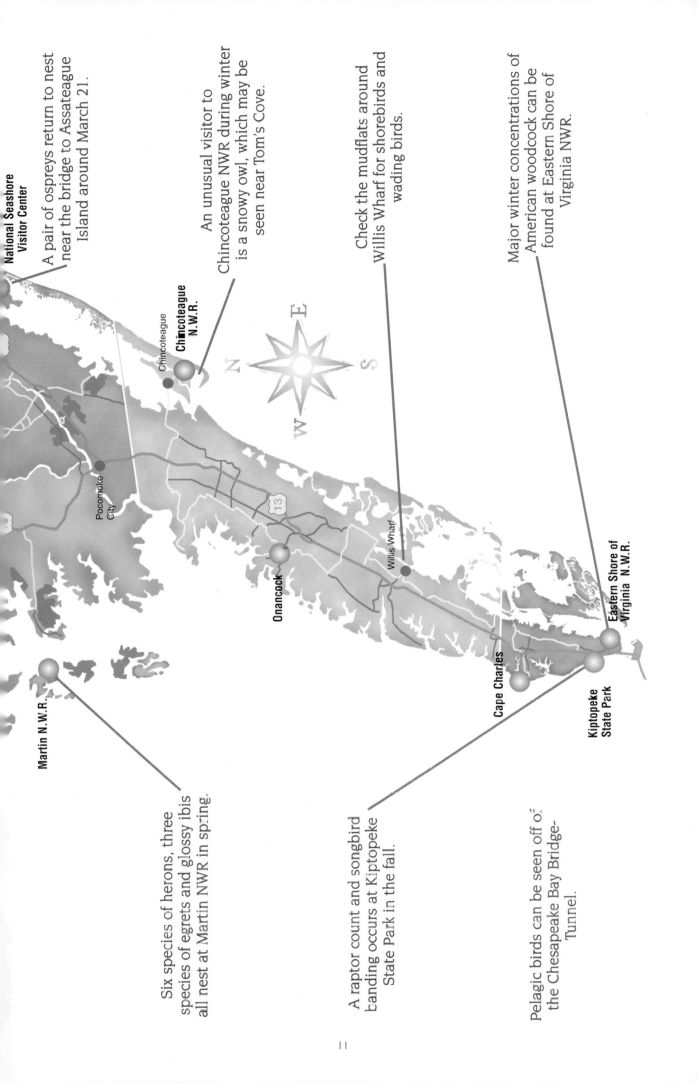

National Seashore Visitor Center

A pair of ospreys return to nest near the bridge to Assateague Island around March 21.

An unusual visitor to Chincoteague NWR during winter is a snowy owl, which may be seen near Tom's Cove.

Check the mudflats around Willis Wharf for shorebirds and wading birds.

Major winter concentrations of American woodcock can be found at Eastern Shore of Virginia NWR.

Chincoteague

Chincoteague N.W.R.

Pocomoke City

Willis Wharf

Onancock

Cape Charles

Eastern Shore of Virginia N.W.R.

Kiptopeke State Park

Martin N.W.R.

Six species of herons, three species of egrets and glossy ibis all nest at Martin NWR in spring.

A raptor count and songbird banding occurs at Kiptopeke State Park in the fall.

Pelagic birds can be seen off of the Chesapeake Bay Bridge-Tunnel.

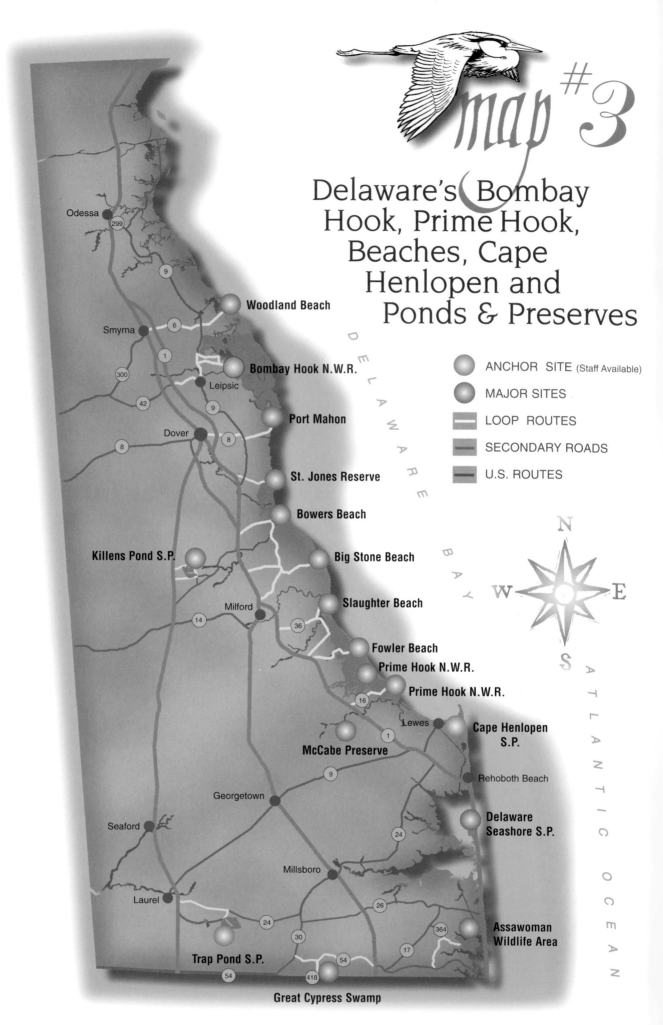

map #3

Delaware's Bombay Hook, Prime Hook, Beaches, Cape Henlopen and Ponds & Preserves

Odessa
299

9

Woodland Beach

Smyrna
6

1
Bombay Hook N.W.R.
300
Leipsic

42
9

Port Mahon

Dover
8
8

St. Jones Reserve

Bowers Beach

Killens Pond S.P.
Big Stone Beach

Milford
Slaughter Beach
14
36

Fowler Beach
Prime Hook N.W.R.
Prime Hook N.W.R.
16

Lewes
Cape Henlopen S.P.
1
McCabe Preserve

9
Rehoboth Beach

Georgetown
Delaware Seashore S.P.
Seaford
24

Millsboro
26
Laurel

24
Assawoman Wildlife Area
30
364
Trap Pond S.P.
17
54
54
418

Great Cypress Swamp

⬤	ANCHOR SITE (Staff Available)	
⬤	MAJOR SITES	
▬	LOOP ROUTES	
▬	SECONDARY ROADS	
▬	U.S. ROUTES	

DELAWARE BAY

ATLANTIC OCEAN

N
W E
S

bombay hook/prime hook

National Wildlife Refuges

Gadwall

ombay Hook is three miles north of the town of Leipsic on Whitehall Neck Road, just off of State Route 9. On entering the refuge, the Visitor Center should be your first stop. You can pick up various brochures, including a bird checklist of 267 species and a list of 70 accidental species. Be sure to check the daily listing of birds other visitors have seen.

Like most National Wildlife Refuges along the East Coast, Bombay Hook was created as a sanctuary for migrating waterfowl. The refuge opened in 1937 and is one of many of that particular vintage that provide a chain of rest stops in the Atlantic Flyway. The shallow freshwater pools and salt marshes attract tens of thousands of geese and ducks, many of which spend the winter here before heading north in the spring.

The refuge attracts more than 100,000 snow geese at the November migration peak, as well as tens of thousands of puddle ducks, diving ducks and Canada geese.

At nearly 16,000 acres, Bombay Hook is a large refuge and today the constituency goes far beyond waterfowl. In spring and summer, the ponds and flats attract thousands of shorebirds and wading birds, including black-necked stilts, glossy ibises, herons, egrets, sandpipers, and plovers. The wooded sections provide an important migratory corridor for warblers, tanagers and other neotropical migrant song-birds. The agricultural fields and grassy meadows attract sparrows, bluebirds, and indigo buntings,

Green Heron

Snow Geese

13

among many others.

The refuge is easily accessible to birders, with a 12-mile auto tour route and five walking trails, three with observation towers. Though October, November, April, and May are the most popular birding months, there really is no off-season when it comes to birding at Bombay Hook. Even in summer, after the spring movement of shore-birds and warblers, and prior to their return in August, there are birds to see. The pools will likely be shallow and reduced in acreage, but if you stay for a while along the edges and patiently scan the flats and wetted areas with binoculars, you're likely to see glossy ibises, black-necked stilts, avocets, semi-palmated sandpipers, least sandpipers, killdeer, yellowlegs, black-crowned night-herons, great blue herons, and great and snowy egrets. It's not uncommon to see a half-dozen black-crowned night-herons perched in a deadfall along Bear Swamp Pool on a July day.

Fall brings the great flocks of waterfowl, for which the refuge is best known. The flights depend upon the weather, beginning in September with teal and continuing through the winter with the arrival of tens of thousands of snow geese.

The shorebirds resume their migration in August, and the neotropical migrant songbirds begin coming through in late August and early

Killdeer
Photo By: Ed Huberty

Black-necked Stilt

September. The songbird migration will continue until November, as great flocks of yellow-rumped warblers gather in the bayberry bushes.

Spring is something of a mirror image of fall, only more colorful and more musical. The male songbirds are in their best nuptial attire and they sing regularly, either to attract a mate, to stake out territory, or to ward off other males. Most people who enjoy songbirds enjoy the spring season because the birds can be identi-fied by song or by plumage. The migration begins as early as March and runs into May.

For more informa-tion, call 302-653-6872, or write to the refuge at 2591 Whitehall Neck Road, Smyrna, DE 19977. The email address is R5RW_BHNWR@mail.fws.gov. The fax number is 302-653-0684.

prime hook

National Wildlife Refuge is an 8,800-acre sanctuary near Milton, Delaware comprised of coastal wetlands, freshwater and tidal salt marshes, and forested and field areas. From Milford, continue south on Rt. 1 to 16 east (Broadkill Beach Road) to 236 - turn left and follow to Visitor Center/ Office.

The refuge was created in 1963 primarily to preserve coastal wetlands for migratory waterfowl. To this end, a system of low dikes was constructed and these pools are

American Avocet

manipulated to stimulate the growth of emergent plants for wildlife use.

As with many other wildlife refuges, however, Prime Hook today caters to a broader constituency. Wading birds, terns, shorebirds, and songbirds all use the refuge, with prime viewing times during the weeks of migration in spring and summer. If it's warblers you want to see, hike the wooded trails of Prime Hook in May or September. Shorebirds are most plentiful in April and May and in late summer

For waterfowl, fall is the time to go. The water control structures will be manipulated to flood 4,200 acres of wetlands, providing excellent habitat

Black-crowned Night-Heron chick

Little Blue Heron

for dabbling ducks. Some species, such as black ducks and wood ducks, nest at Prime Hook, but most of the birds you will see during the winter months are migrants. Depending upon the severity of the winter, some will spend the winter on or near the refuge; others will head farther south.

Prime Hook is an excel-

Great Blue Heron

15

Ring-necked Pheasant

lent place to go birding by boat. So bring your canoe and paddle more than 15 miles of streams such as Prime Hook Creek, Slaughter Canal and Petersfield Ditch. Several boat launch ramps are available to provide easy access.

A self-guided canoe trail begins at Waples Mill Pond and extends some seven miles to the refuge office. You can either paddle out and back, or park a second vehicle at the take-out point. From October 15 to March 15, the lower three miles are closed. This canoe trip provides a close look at the wetlands and the birds they support. Depending upon the season, expect to see a variety of waterfowl, shorebirds, and wading birds such as herons and egrets. Songbirds will be seen in the forested areas.

A boardwalk interpretive trail was constructed by the Youth Conservation Corps in 1974, and although it is less than a mile long, it covers a wide

Northern Cardinal

range of habitat, from an old fruit orchard to a family cemetery to marshland and woodland communities. The boardwalk trail is especially productive during the spring and fall songbird migrations, when a wide variety of warblers, thrushes, tanagers, and resident birds can be seen.

For information, contact the refuge at RD#3, Box 195, Milton, Delaware 19968. Phone 302-684-8419.

Blue Jays

Laughing Gulls with Horseshoe Crabs

Delaware has numerous beaches where public access is allowed, from Cape Henlopen, which separates the Delaware Bay from the Atlantic, to Woodland Beach, where the Delaware River enters the bay. In between, there are numerous protected areas interspersed with residential communities, so if you visit these beaches, please stick to the public areas and observe the rights of private property owners.

South of Cape Henlopen are the ocean beaches - Rehoboth, Dewey, Bethany, Fenwick - and, although much of the beach property has undergone recreational and residential development, this area offers a unique opportunity for birders, especially during fall and winter when the waterfowl are passing through and sea ducks and pelagic birds are passing offshore.

Here is a selection of Delaware beaches where public access is allowed and the birding opportunities are varied, from sea ducks to shorebirds. Refer to the map on page 12 for specific directions.

Barred Owl
Photo By: Ed Huberty

delaware seashore

State Park, south of Dewey Beach, is a welcome expanse of wild beach, dunes, and salt marsh straddling Rt. 1. The park, the visitor center of which is on the north side of Indian River Inlet, offers both ocean and bay access. The ocean beach is a great venue for watching sea ducks from October through the winter. Northern

American Wigeon

17

gannets can usually be seen flying south in the fall, occasionally making a spectacular dive at an unsuspecting trout or bluefish. Great flocks of scoters and oldsquaw fly just above the surface of the ocean.

On the bay side of the barrier island strip, Burtons Island trail provides a look at waterfowl in fall and winter, plus migrating songbirds in spring and fall. Look for wading birds in the shallow ponds, sharp-tailed sparrows in the marsh south of the campground.

silver lake

in Rehoboth is a good place to see waterfowl, especially canvasbacks, from November to late March. Monk parakeets nest along the north side of the lake. Look for the stick nest atop a telephone pole on the left side of the pond. The lake is off Robinson Street in south Rehoboth. A small parking lot provides access.

Northern Gannet

cape henlopen
State Park

near Lewes means many things to many people. Its history includes America's seafaring past, national defense, and a long tradition of public use. In 1682, William Penn declared that the lands of the Cape were for the common use of the citizens of Lewes and Sussex County, thus establishing the nation's first public lands. Cape Henlopen served as a military base during World War II, and for centuries the old lighthouse and breakwater provided guidance and safe harbor for sailors.

For birders, Cape Henlopen offers a wide range of habitats and, consequently, a wide range of birds. The bay side of the spit that separates bay and ocean is a good place to see horseshoe crabs and shorebirds during the spring

Northern Flicker

migration. Portions of this beach are closed during nesting season, but the parking lot at the end of Cape Henlopen Drive offers an excellent view.

Don't miss the biking/hiking trails that begin at the amphitheater parking lot and run along the dunes to a lookout atop one of the highest dunes in the park. The dunes provide a great view of the beach and are perfect for hawk watching in the fall.

The wooded areas are productive for

Snowy Owl, Immature

18

migrating songbirds in April/May and September/October. Waterfowl are plentiful on Gordon's Pond in fall and winter. There often are surprises such as snowy owls in the sand dunes in winter and flocks of snow buntings patrolling the beach.

The Nature Center near the park entrance can provide details on recent sightings and they offer birding tours led by staff naturalists. If you're new to the area, a guided trip would be a good idea. While you're at the Nature Center, check out the feeding stations. There often are some surprise birds along with the chickadees and titmice.

Carolina Chickadee

American Oystercatchers
Photo By: Ed Huberty

As an interesting side trip, take a ride on the Cape May-Lewes Ferry. A variety of gulls are usually in attendance and in winter you can watch sea ducks and, perhaps, pick up a few pelagic species.

Follow Rd. 16 east from Rt. 1 and you'll cross Prime Hook National Wildlife Refuge and end up at Broadkill Beach. A left turn along the way (see the sign) will take you to the refuge headquarters and visitor center, where there are hiking trails, a canoe trail, and a helpful staff to provide information. One of the best birding spots in the area is the shallow wetland along the causeway just west of the beach. A hard shoulder area provides off-road parking and the ponds will provide a look at various shorebirds and wading birds during spring and

late summer and waterfowl in the fall and winter. A spotting scope with a window mount would be a good idea here.

Broadkill is essentially a residential community of summer homes, with Beach Plum Island Nature Preserve, south of the residential community, providing public access. A parking area is provided and there are paths across the dunes to the beach which provide easy access for surf fishers and for those who simply want to explore the beach. It's an excellent venue for horseshoe crab/shorebird watching in May

Eastern Screech Owl

and early June.

The beaches here are narrow spits with a sandy berm, low dunes, and vegetated communities consisting of cedar, wild black cherry, bayberry, and beach plum. A wide expanse of marsh separates the beach from the mainland. Most of the marshland and contiguous upland are included in Prime Hook NWR.

fowler beach

is a few miles north of Broadkill at the end of Rd. 199 and is surrounded by Prime Hook NWR. The road provides a nice overlook of the salt marsh, including some stands of phragmites that are being reverted to spartina marshes. The road ends at the beach with just enough room to turn around. The beach is popular for fishing and provides a good habitat for horseshoe crabs to lay their eggs at high tide, and for shorebirds that feed on the eggs at low tide.

Boat-tailed Grackle
Photo By: Ed Huberty

Great Egret

to early spring, waterfowl are present on the bay and in the marsh. Look for short-eared owls over the marsh at dawn and dusk.

From late summer to early spring, a number of rare gulls can be seen at Mispillion Inlet. Look for Franklin's gulls in late summer and little and black-headed gulls from fall to early spring. In May, shorebirds feed on horseshoe crab eggs. Waterfowl are abundant in winter.

To reach Mispillion Inlet, take Rt. 1 to Rt. 36 in Milford. Take Rt. 36 east to CR 203. Turn left on CR 203 and follow it to the end.

slaughter beach

From the north, take Rt. 1 to Rt. 36 in Milford. Take Rt. 36 east until it ends in the town of Slaughter Beach. Many streets on the left offer access to the Delaware Bay beaches. From the south, take Rt. 1 to CR 224. Take CR 224 west to the end. Streets on the right provide access to Bay beaches.

Slaughter Beach provides a good spot to observe shorebirds during the spring migration. In May and early June, horseshoe crabs spawn on high tides and shorebirds feed on the eggs at low tide. From fall

Red-shouldered Hawk

milford neck

and Big Stone Beach are good places to watch shorebirds in spring and summer. You should see a variety of wading birds such as herons and egrets, shorebirds, rails and marsh sparrows, plus migrant songbirds in wooded areas. In fall, waterfowl, raptors, and migrating songbirds appear. Waterfowl and raptors often remain over winter.

To get there, take Rt. 113 to CR 19 - Thompsonville Rd., turn left on CR 425, Big Stone Beach Rd., and follow it to the end.

bowers beach

is another small residential beach community with a marina, boat launch facility, stores and a few restaurants. Most of the beach is private, but there is a good beach overlook at the north end of the community. Parking is limited and there is soft sand off the road, so be careful.

Just north, across the creek, is state-owned Ted Harvey Conservation Area, another good birding location.

port mahon,

east of Dover, consists of farmland, forest, salt marsh, and bayshore. Much of it is protected, either by federal, state, or private conservation organizations. Bombay Hook NWR includes about 16,000 acres, and south of that is Little Creek Wildlife Area, which is owned by the state. The Nature Conservancy owns the 340-acre Port Mahon Preserve, at the end of Rt. 8 on the Mahon River, a 1990 gift from Conectiv, formerly Delmarva Power.

Access is via Rd. 8 off Rt. 9 south of

Yellow-bellied Sapsucker

Dover, just outside of the town of Little Creek. The road runs along the bayshore, with a marsh and phragmites stands to the north, and ends at the Conservancy's preserve and a parking area with boat launch facilities. Along the way, beach birds can be seen, although much of the shoreline has been covered with riprap to prevent the road from washing out, so it's not exactly prime horseshoe crab nesting habitat. Crab eggs do wash into the area with the tides, however, attracting birds, so the Mahon area is well worth checking out in May for shorebirds.

Pied-billed Grebe

Hiking trails are available at the preserve, but insects can be bothersome during the warm season, so be prepared.

woodland beach

is sandwiched between Bombay Hook NWR and Woodland Beach Wildlife Area, which is managed by the state. It is a small beach community with a public launch ramp, fishing pier, and parking area. The pier provides a good look at the shoreline, as well as the open water. Most of the shoreline here is peaty or lined with phragmites thickets, so it's not the best horseshoe crab/shorebird habitat.

The pier should provide a good view of sea ducks and other open water birds in winter.

Woodland Beach is reached via Rt. 6 east of Smyrna. A small boat launch area on the left just west of the beach provides a good put-in for those wishing to explore the marshes by canoe or small boat.

Eastern Kingbird

delaware ponds and preserves

Delaware is perhaps best known among birders for its hundreds of miles of shoreline and its vast bayshore wildlife refuges such as Bombay Hook and Prime Hook. But for warbler watching in spring and fall, Delaware's upland offers numerous parks and wildlife areas where the birding is among the best on Delmarva. There also are parks and wildlife areas near the coast that provide a good look at wetlands birds such as rails, wading birds, and water-loving warblers such as prothonotaries and common yellowthroats.

What follows are some of Delaware's state parks, forests, and wildlife areas, and the birds you're likely to see there at different times of the year.

Red-shouldered Hawks

Great-Crested Flycatcher

the best times. Wood ducks nest on the pond, and prothonotary warblers can often be spotted near the water. Prothonotaries, acadian flycatchers, and summer tanagers nest in the park. The forested areas also have barred owls and pileated woodpeckers. Look for red-shouldered hawks in the open areas.

trap pond

State Park is about 10 miles east of Laurel. Take Rt. 24 to CR 449 and turn right. The park entrance is about one mile south on the south side of the pond.

The wooded area is a good place to see migrating songbirds in spring and fall, with April/May and September /October being

Barred Owl

great cypress swamp

straddles the Maryland-Delaware line, west of Selbyville on Rt. 54. The swamp offers excellent birding for migratory species during the spring and fall seasons. There are no public facilities, but a walk along the roadside in the forested area will usually turn up some interesting migratory and nesting species, including worm-eating and prothonotary warblers, yellow-throated and Kentucky warblers, Louisiana waterthrush, blue-gray gnatcatcher, Acadian flycatcher, and others.

assawoman

Wildlife Area is northeast of Selbyville on CR 364, and it offers good birding year round. Brown-headed nuthatches are residents, and migratory songbirds can be seen in spring and fall. Many species can be observed by walking along the roadsides through the wildlife area.

st jones reserve

is southeast of Dover Air Force Base on Kitts Hummock Road. Its 700 acres include a variety of habitats and birds, including shorebirds, raptors, owls, wading birds, waterfowl, and nesting songbirds.

ted harvey

Conservation Area abuts the St. Jones Reserve, and its 2,000 acres provide important nesting and resting habitat for a wide variety of birds, including wading birds, shorebirds, waterfowl, and migrating songbirds. Upland sandpipers can be seen in the fields along Rt. 9 north of Kitts Hummock Rd.

killens pond

State Park north of Milford offers a wide variety of habitat and a corresponding variety of birds. The freshwater pond will have waterfowl in fall and early winter, including wood ducks, which nest

Red-breasted Nuthatch

Wood Ducks

Pileated Woodpecker

there, and teal. Prothonotary warblers and Acadian flycatchers are common nesters. The wooded areas will have migratory songbirds in spring and fall.

edward h. mccabe

Preserve is a Nature Conservancy Preserve along the banks of the Broadkill River, south of Milton. Take Rd. 88 4.4 miles from Rt. 1 to Rd. 257 and turn right. The Preserve parking lot is located .7 miles ahead on the left. From the lot, a 3-mile trail traverses 143 acres of forest, fields and riverside wetlands. Birding is best in May when neotropical migrant songbirds stop to rest and feed along their northward journey. Nesting birds include yellow-breasted chats, prothonotary warblers, wood ducks and wood thrushes. Sit quietly on a riverside bench and you are likely to see great blue herons, common yellowthroats and possibly hunting bald eagles. In fall and winter, the woods harbor busy flocks of chickadees, titmice and kinglets. Hermit thrushes are common winter residents in the dense woodland understory. Throughout the winter the huge, noisy flocks of snow geese pass overhead on their way to and from the nearby Prime Hook NWR. For a dash of adventure, launch a canoe in downtown Milton, paddle a mile to the preserve dock and then hike below the Preserve's forest canopy.

map #4

Maryland's Upper Shore

ANCHOR SITE (Staff Available)

MAJOR SITES

LOOP ROUTES

SECONDARY ROADS

U.S. ROUTES

N
W E
S

CHESAPEAKE BAY

Chester River

213

20

300

213

301

445

Eastern Neck
N.W.R.

Horsehead
Wetlands Center

Wye Island N.R.M.A.

Pickering Creek
Environmental Center

404

Tuckahoe S.P.

Denton

Martinak S.P.

Choptank River

Easton

33

322

331

50

maryland's upper shore

Canada geese, rolling fields of corn, and crabcakes at a dockside restaurant. These are the things that have made Maryland's northern Eastern Shore well known throughout the world.

Drive the back roads near Easton in the fall, or head up to Chestertown and out to Rock Hall, and in nearly every mile you'll see Canada geese hanging over cornfields in ragged lines. Stop the car, roll down the window, and listen to the goose music; it chills the spine, a harbinger of winter.

Maryland's upper Eastern Shore lacks the massive wildlife refuges we find elsewhere on Delmarva, but there are many excellent public birding sites, some federally owned, some state property, and several that are operated by private conservation groups.

For this guide, we consider the northern Eastern Shore roughly the area north of the Choptank River up the bayshore to the Sassafras River and the C.&D. Canal. Here are some outstanding birding areas on the northern Eastern Shore.

Turkey Vulture
Photo By: Ed Huberty

easton

is known worldwide for its fall Waterfowl Festival and for the attendant local traditions of hunting and wildfowl art. A trip to the Easton area in the fall is one of life's great pleasures.

Canada Goose

Tricolored Heron
Photo By: Ed Huberty

pickering creek

Environmental Center

is worth a visit any time of year for any true birder. You'll see waterfowl in fall and winter, but spring and early fall bring great concentrations of songbirds such as warblers, vireos, tanagers, and thrushes.

The Pickering Creek center is operated by the Chesapeake Audubon Society and includes 400 acres of woodland, upland, and wetland. Traveling west on Rt. 50, turn left at Airport Road in Easton, then immediately turn right onto Rt. 662 (Longwoods Rd.). Follow Rt. 662 to Sharp Rd., turn left, then the second

Downy Woodpecker/Male

Female

right and the center will be on your right. (See sign.)

A hiking trail covers a wide variety of habitat and offers especially good birding in spring and fall. The head of the trail is near the center office. A mixed hardwood forest at the beginning of the trail is prime songbird habitat. A variety of woodpeckers also live in the woods, as do barred and great horned owls. Look for Eastern towhees in the undergrowth.

The trail crosses several bogs and winds along the banks of the creek, where waterfowl and wading birds can be seen. It ends at the farm equipment sheds, where a demonstration garden is maintained.

Instead of retracing your steps to return to the trail head, walk back along the gravel road. There often are hawks hunting over the corn fields and bluebirds along the field edges. In fall, great numbers of yellow-rumped warblers can be seen in this edge habitat where farm field, shrub, and forest meet.

One of the best birding spots is the bus parking lot, which is along the field edge just as the road enters the woods near the office building. The sun is at your back during most daylight hours here, making it easier to see detail and color. There is a large walnut tree along the edge, along with numerous plants and shrubs preferred by birds. Ruby-crowned kinglets are plentiful in these shrubs in fall.

Pickering Creek offers naturalist-led group trips for schools, families, and adult groups. Call 410-822-4903 for information.

wye island

Natural Resources Management Area is a short drive west on Rt. 50 from Easton, turn left at Carmichael, and visit this state sanctuary on the Wye River. Fall and winter are the best times to visit, as waterfowl will be plentiful on the open water and in the marshes.

American Wigeons

horsehead

Wetlands Center, a 500-acre sanctuary of wetlands, upland, and shallow ponds, is a bit farther along Rt. 50, near the town of Grasonville. The center is operated by the Wildfowl Trust of North America, a non-profit organization the mission of which is to preserve wildfowl and wetlands through education, conservation, and research. The center is just outside of Grasonville. From east bound Rt. 50 take exit 43B. From west bound Rt. 50 take exit 44A, onto Rt. 18 and follow the signs to the center.

Not surprisingly, you'll see many waterfowl here, including a captive collection. In fall and winter, the numbers swell with migrating birds, which flock to the shallow ponds, or to the open waters of Eastern Bay.

A number of hiking trails lead to several constructed ponds, with observation blinds and platforms providing excellent venues. Portions of the trails cross wooded areas, where songbirds can be seen. Bald eagles nest near the sanctuary and can sometimes be seen soaring above the wetlands.

For information, phone 410-827-6694.

Sharp-shinned Hawk

eastern neck

National Wildlife Refuge is but a short hop across the Chester River from Horsehead, as the eagle flies. Lacking the flight capabilities of the eagle, however, we humans must travel back east on Rt. 50, then north on Rt. 213 to Chestertown, south on Rt. 20 to Rock Hall, and finally south again on Rt. 445 to the refuge. We'll cover more than 50 miles to reach a point about five miles north of where we previously stood.

But Eastern Neck is well worth the drive. The terrain of Queen Anne's and Kent Counties takes on a subtle roll, corn fields stretch for miles, and waterfront towns such as Rock Hall offer unpretentious hospitality and spicy crabcakes.

Oh yes, and birds. Visit in the fall, roll down the window, and listen to those Canada geese as they glide in to feast on corn. From Rock Hall, Rt. 445 will take you across a narrow bridge and onto Eastern Neck Island, a 2,285-acre refuge the major constituency of which is wildfowl. An estimated 40,000 ducks and geese spend the winter on or near the refuge, including great flocks of canvasbacks. Dabbling ducks such as blacks, mallards, and wigeons can be seen in shallows, with diving ducks present in the deeper open waters.

Eastern Phoebe

The refuge also has about 500 acres of forest and 100 acres of grassland, so it provides a good opportunity to see songbirds during the spring and fall migrations, as well as resident species. Southern bald eagles nest on the refuge as well. Three hiking trails provide access to good birding habitat, and a boat ramp at Bogles Wharf Landing is handy for those who like to do their birding by boat. Phone 410-639-7056 for information.

Arboretum. Lake Trail begins at the lake, where there usually are a few waterfowl, and runs along the headwaters of Tuckahoe Creek to a picnic area. The trail is less than a mile long, but it covers a variety of habitat, beginning in a pine woods, extending along some vegetated wetlands and into an upland hardwood forest, and finally entering a shrub thicket near the picnic area. Songbirds are abundant during migrations, and there are numerous resident species year-round.

For information, call 410-820-1668.

tuckahoe

State Park near Denton, at 3,800 acres, offers a wealth of outdoor opportunities, from fishing and camping to birdwatching. The park is seven miles west of Denton, north of the junction of Rts. 404 and 480. From Rt. 480 veer left on Eveland Road, follow signs. Tuckahoe Creek runs through the park.

A number of hiking trails provide access to good birding habitat. Piney Branch Trail connects the picnic area with Adkins

Eastern Bluebird

adkins arboretum

is in Tuckahoe State Park, and while the mission of the arboretum is to preserve and propagate native plant species, it is an excellent place for birdwatching. The arboretum is a short distance north of the state park office on Eveland Road off Rt. 480.

A visitors center offers information, interpretive displays, and a gallery. An interpretive trail begins behind the center, runs through a hardwood forest, along a forested wetland, and then skirts an open meadow, providing a wealth of different habitat in less than a mile. An excellent interpretive guide is available for loan in the mailbox at the trail hea, and a bird list can be obtained at the visitors center.

The wooded areas provide opportunities to see visiting songbirds during migration, with April and May and September and October the peak months. Residents include woodpeckers, towhees, chickadees, titmice, and numerous others.

If you want to birdwatch along the interpretive trail, consider hiking it in reverse order. That is, instead of heading into the woods at the trail head, walk instead along the meadow. This way, the sun will be at your back as you scan this important edge habitat that separates grassland, shrub, and forest. Those warblers and sparrows are confusing enough without having to view them silhouetted against the sun.

Red-tailed Hawk

For more information on the arboretum, call 410-634-2847.

martinak

State Park also is located off Rt. 404, on Deep Shore Road two miles south of Denton. It's a relatively small park at 107 acres, but its wooded frontage on Watts Creek and the Choptank River make it an excellent birding destination. A boat ramp is available if you want to explore by water.

A loop fitness trail is located near the park entrance and a nature trail runs from the information booth near the entrance to the edge of Watts Creek on the southern edge of the park. Both trails provide good birding, especially during those spring and fall migration windows.

The phone number at the park office is 410-820-1668.

Common Yellowthroat

Maryland's Middle Shore

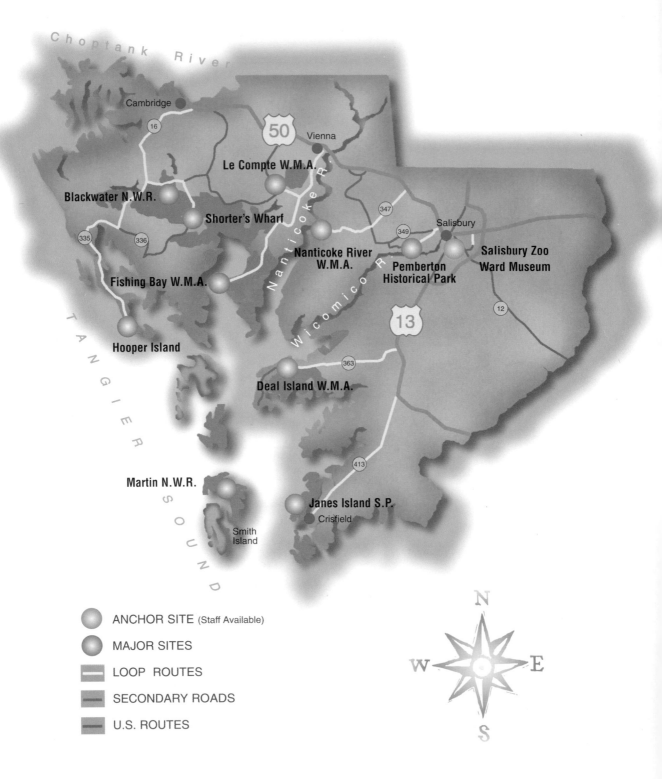

Choptank River

Cambridge

16

50

Vienna

Le Compte W.M.A.

Blackwater N.W.R.

Shorter's Wharf

347

349

Salisbury

Nanticoke River
W.M.A.

Pemberton
Historical Park

Salisbury Zoo
Ward Museum

335

336

Fishing Bay W.M.A.

13

12

Hooper Island

363

Deal Island W.M.A.

TANGIER SOUND

413

Martin N.W.R.

Janes Island S.P.

Crisfield

Smith
Island

⬤ ANCHOR SITE (Staff Available)

⬤ MAJOR SITES

▬ LOOP ROUTES

▬ SECONDARY ROADS

▬ U.S. ROUTES

N
W E
S

maryland's middle shore

Maryland's middle Eastern Shore includes some of the most diverse habitat on Delmarva. The Chesapeake Bay lies on the western edge of this section and, with it, some of the Shore's largest rivers: the Choptank, Nanticoke, and Wicomico. Blackwater National Wildlife Refuge has thousands of acres of marsh and impoundments that attract great flocks of ducks and geese.

Inland, there are wildlife management areas that offer a combination of forests, wetlands, open fields and meadows, so, on the middle shore you're likely to see everything from canvasbacks to nesting warblers. Here are some of the best bets for birding on Maryland's middle Eastern Shore.

Redheads

Short-eared Owl

hooper island

lies at the end of Rt. 335 southwest of Cambridge. It's bordered on the west by the Chesapeake Bay and on the east by the Honga River. Not surprisingly, a drive to Hooper Island in fall or winter will provide a good look at many waterfowl species.

The area also has a resident population of bald eagles, and a colony of great blue herons and great egrets nests offshore on Barren Island (part of Blackwater NWR). There are gulls, terns, shorebirds, and many diving ducks in the winter.

choptank river

provides good waterfowl viewing from late fall through early spring. The wider sections near Cambridge may have tundra swans, oldsquaw, common goldeneye, canvasbacks, and redheads. The Cambridge Municipal Basin and Yacht Club parking lot overlooks the river and provides good viewing, as does Great Marsh Point at the end of Somerset Avenue.

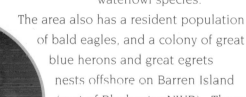

Mallard/female

blackwater

National Wildlife Refuge near Cambridge is the best place on Delmarva to see bald eagles. The refuge has the largest nesting population on the East Coast north of Florida. The refuge has more than 23,000 acres of marsh, with large areas of open water, and woodlands with a loop road and a few trails. There is a chance of seeing golden eagles in winter, plus Ross', snow and greater white-fronted geese.

A wide variety of other birds are found year-round, especially herons, waterfowl, raptors and shorebirds. Breeding species include black-necked stilts, summer tanagers, blue grosbeaks, grasshopper sparrows, chuck-will's-widows, and brown-headed nuthatches. Endangered Delmarva fox squirrels are present year-round.

For more information, call the Visitor Center at Blackwater NWR at 410-228-2677.

A possible side trip from Blackwater NWR would be the Shorter's Wharf Boat Ramp. From the entrance to Blackwater NWR Wildlife Drive, take Key Wallace Rd. 1 mile east, turn right onto Maple Dam Rd., travel about 5.5 miles to the boat ramp beside the bridge over Blackwater River. Tens of thousands of acres of brackish-water marsh can be accessed from this ramp.

Yellow Warbler

black), and in winter, look for raptors (including rough-legged hawks, northern harriers, short-eared owls) and waterfowl.

For more information, contact the Maryland DNR at 410-376-3236.

le compte Wildlife Management Area

is on Steele's Neck Road southwest of Vienna. It's a good example of a mature mixed hardwood/loblolly pine forest. Established as a refuge for the Delmarva

fishing bay Wildlife Management Area,

also known as the Elliott Island marshes, lies on a peninsula between Fishing Bay and the Nanticoke River. From the town of Vienna, Henry's Crossroads Road and Elliott Island Road lead southwest to the WMA and a boat ramp on Fishing Bay.

The marshes along the road are good in spring and early summer for breeding sparrows (seaside & sharp-tailed), marsh wrens & rails (including

Common Nighthawk

fox squirrel, this endangered species can be found here as well as wild turkeys, pileated woodpeckers and a variety of upland forest and shrub species. Northern pintails, green-winged teal and other waterfowl frequent the ponds in late winter. The WMA has two parking lots and hiking trails.

For more information, contact MD DNR at 410-376-3236.

Marsh Road near Vienna passes through a field (possible blue grosbeaks) and then forested area (wood thrushes, vireos) and then opens up onto marshes along the Nanticoke River. Nesting species include ospreys, king rails, wood ducks, orchard orioles, and yellow warblers. Waterfowl and eagles are found here in winter.

Northern Pintails

nanticoke river

Wildlife Management Area

is west of Quantico, at the end of Nutter's Neck Road. Birding is good from fall through early summer. This area includes a variety of habitats including mixed hardwood/pine forest, loblolly pine stands, forested wetlands, fresh and brackish marshes, and agricultural fields. It's a good spot for raptors, wild turkeys, and a variety of songbirds, especially sparrows.

For more information, contact the Maryland DNR at 410-543-8223.

Bald Eagle

The park has historical attractions, hiking trails, and a convenience building with restrooms, park information, and a bird checklist. Birding is good year-round at Pemberton. The park includes approximately five miles of trails which traverse a number of habitats supporting a variety of nesting songbirds (including scarlet tanagers, prothonotary warblers and white-eyed vireos), bald eagles, barred owls, and osprey. In winter, look for a variety of raptors and waterfowl.

Historic Pemberton Hall (1741) and the museum of the Wicomico

pemberton

Historical Park is located on the Western side of Salisbury. To get there from downtown Salisbury, travel on Rt. 50 West to Rt. 349 (Nanticoke Road). Turn left on Nanticoke Road and take the next immediate left onto Pemberton Drive. Travel approximately 2 miles, Pemberton Historical Park is on the left.

Summer Tanager

County Historical Society are also located in the park.

For more information, call 410-860-2447 or the Wicomico County Dept. of Recreation and Parks at 410-548-4900.

ward museum

of Wildfowl Art is on Schumaker Pond on Beaglin Park Drive in Salisbury. This unique museum offers an extensive collection of antique hunting decoys and contemporary bird carvings. It is open daily.

Schumaker Pond can be viewed from the museum and from a trail along the shoreline. In winter, a variety of waterfowl, including ring-necked ducks, wigeon, and tundra swans, are found on the pond. Breeding species include wood ducks, red-bellied woodpeckers, and scarlet tanagers.

For more information, call the Ward Museum at 410-742-4988.

salisbury zoological park

on South Park Drive in Salisbury, is widely regarded as one of North America's finest small zoos. The zoo is free and open daily, and specializes in the display of species native to the western hemisphere. Birds of North and South America are maintained in naturalistic outdoor exhibits, including such Delmarva species as bald eagles, various local owls and an impressive collection of North American waterfowl.

Seasonal visitors such as cedar waxwings and ruby-throated hummingbirds can be

seen feeding in the Donald Bridgwater Bird and Butterfly Garden near the zoo office. Other wild inhabitants seen with some regularity include pileated woodpeckers, white-breasted nuthatches and belted kingfishers. Birding opportunities also exist along the Salisbury Urban Greenway, a rustic forest trail that connects the Salisbury Zoo to the Ward Museum of Wildfowl Art.

For more information, call the Salisbury Zoo at 410-548-3188.

deal island

Wildlife Management Area is on Rt. 363, ten miles west of Princess Anne in Somerset County. Two dirt roads (which should be driven with caution) provide access into the WMA. The first entrance is on the left side of Rt. 363, approximately one mile past the town of St. Stephens, and is marked by a large refuge sign. This road continues approximately 1.5 miles to a parking area. To reach the second road into the western end of the refuge, return to Rt.363, turn left and continue approximately 1.5 miles to Riley Roberts Rd., turn left onto it and follow it past a small settlement at which point the road becomes dirt, enters the refuge, and continues about 2.5 miles, ending at a parking lot.

Extensive fresh to brackish marshes with some

American Kestrel

Common Loon

adjoining woodlands provides very good to excellent birding from the two dirt roads throughout the year. Winter residents and visitors include bald eagles, short-eared owls, northern harriers, rough-legged hawks, tundra swans, and a variety of ducks.

Migrants include a number of shorebirds, and nesting species include black-necked stilts, sharp-tailed and seaside sparrows, marsh wrens, clapper, Virginia and black rails. Light conditions for birding from the Riley Roberts Road extension are best in the afternoon.

For more information, contact the Maryland DNR at 410-543-8223.

janes island

State Park has several distinct areas for birdwatchers to enjoy. A developed mainland section along Daugherty Creek canal offers trails and a resident naturalist. Another portion of the park is accessible by boat and provides water activity opportunities, miles of isolated shorelines and marsh areas, which delight

Wild Turkey

martin

National Wildlife Refuge encompasses over 4,000 acres on the northern half of Smith Island, which lies 11 miles west of Crisfield, Maryland, in the lower Chesapeake Bay. The refuge is closed to the general public to protect nesting and wintering wildlife. However, birdwatchers can cruise slowly along the shoreline, and view many species of waterfowl, wading birds, shorebirds, herons, egrets and the glossy ibis nesting together in several rookeries on the refuge. The area also supports small populations of marsh animals, fox, muskrat, otter, etc. Several threatened and endangered species occasionally stop at the refuge, including bald eagles that nest on Martin NWR. Ospreys have nested at the refuge for years, and nesting towers have been installed to assist in the growing peregrine falcon population. The refuge visitor center, located on Smith Island in the town of Ewell, is open from April to November, with information and exhibits. The area is accessible only by boat. For transportation or refuge information, call 800-521-9189 or 410-425-4971.

Barn Swallow

visitors who enjoy natural areas. The park is located on Tangier Sound in Crisfield, Maryland and may be reached by Rt. 13 south, to Rt.413, and right onto Rt. 358. For more information, you can call 410-968-1565.

Red-winged Blackbird

map #6
Maryland's Lower Shore

Great Cypress Swamp

610

368

50

Isle of Wight W.M.A.

354

90

Elliott's Pond

Adkins Mill

Powellville

374

Berlin

Ocean City

376

611

Whiton's Crossing

113

Assateague Island
National Seashore
Visitor Center

12

354

611

Porter's Crossing

Furnace Town

Red House Rd.
Canoe Launch

Pocomoke River

Snow Hill

Pocomoke River State Park

E.A. Vaughn W.M.A.

Pocomoke City

12

13

CHINCOTEAGUE BAY

N
W   E
S

ANCHOR SITE (Staff Available)

MAJOR SITES

LOOP ROUTES

SECONDARY ROADS

U.S. ROUTES

maryland's lower shore

Maryland's lower Eastern Shore offers a wealth of natural diversity. Thousands of acres are protected by the state as Pocomoke River State Forest, where extensive cypress forests provide breeding habitat to prothonotary warblers, woodpeckers, vireos, and many other species. The Nature Conservancy owns a preserve along Nassawango Creek, a tributary of the Pocomoke, where a day spent in a canoe can turn up all sorts of birding and botanical gems

To cap it off, we have the seaside bays, tidal flats, and the open waters of the Atlantic. So a day spent birding in Worcester County could turn up everything from warblers to sea ducks. Here are some of the best places to visit.

Cormorants

A walk along the park roads usually provides good birding, with ovenbirds, blue-gray gnatcatchers, and various other species. The fishing pond across from the boat ramp is a good place to bird, and perhaps the best area is the Trail of Change, a loop that covers a mature hardwood forest, re-forested farmland, and cypress swamp.

Nesting birds include brown-headed nuthatches (year-round residents) and prothonotary, yellow-throated and other warblers (summer residents).

For more information, call Pocomoke State Forest at 410-632-2566.

Tree Swallow

shad landing

Pocomoke River State Park

is on Rt. 113 south of Snow Hill. The park office near the entrance has information on interpretive nature trails here and at the Milburn Landing site on the other side of the river. A Nature Center is open during the summer, and canoe rentals and camping spaces are available

American Redstart

c. a. vaughn
Wildlife Management

Area is on Rt. 12 between Stockton and Girdletree. This state WMA includes a variety of upland (open and wooded) and wetland (fresh and salt) habitats, attracting migrants, wintering and nesting species. Notable species include pied-billed grebe, least bittern, common moorhen, brown-headed nuthatch, grasshopper sparrow, orchard oriole and blue grosbeak.

For more information, contact the Maryland DNR at 410-543-8223.

bog-ore furnace. The head of the Paul Leifer Nature Trail is located close to the furnace ruins.

The trail is approximately one mile through the Pocomoke Forest and the Nassawango Cypress Swamp. A variety of neotropical migrants breed here including prothonotary, worm-eating and Kentucky warblers, summer and scarlet tanagers and Acadian and great crested flycatchers.

Furnace Town's grounds and the Nature Conservancy Paul Leifer Trail are available for birding and walking during daylight hours; an admission fee is charged from April 1 through October 31 between 11 a.m. and 5 p.m. Free admission with presentation of valid Nature Conservancy or Furnace Town membership card.

Another accessible spot along Nassawango Creek good for observing summer resident neotropical species (including scarlet tanager, Acadian flycatcher, redstart, Louisiana waterthrush, prothonotary, yellow-throated, hooded and Kentucky warblers), is from Mt. Olive Church Rd. where it crosses the creek. From Old Furnace Rd. turn left on Rt. 12, after 1/2 mile, turn right onto Mt. Olive Church Rd, after about 4 miles, look for wooden bridge over the creek (and The Nature Conservancy signs). Park along side of road and bird from the road.

American Goldfinch

red house road

Canoe Launch for Nassawango Creek

is 2.5 miles west of Rt. 12 north of Snow Hill. It's a great spot for a birding trip via canoe, or you can simply check out the forested area in the vicinity of the Nassawango Creek bridge.

Canoeing south from the launch takes you through woodland habitat good for warblers and other neotropical species in spring and summer. Waterfowl can be observed in spring and fall. Canoeing to the southeast approximately 1.5 miles leads to the Pocomoke River from which the trip can be continued south to Shad Landing State Park or north to the Snow Hill parks.

Belted Kingfisher

porter's crossing

is a popular canoe launch site on the Pocomoke River about five miles north (by water) of Snow Hill. Porter's Crossing Road intersects with Rt. 113, 3.75 miles north of Snow Hill and the launch site is at the bridge about one mile from the intersection.

furnace town

— Paul Leifer Nature Trail is 2.5 miles off Rt. 12 on Old Furnace Road north of Snow Hill. There is a charge for going into the historic site, which is an interesting mid-19th century village involved with the production of iron using a

American Wigeons & American Coots

The Pocomoke is narrow at Porter's Crossing and it winds through a picturesque swamp beneath a canopy of trees. It becomes broad 5 miles downstream at the Snow Hill Parks. A canoe trip in spring and fall will turn up various neotropical migrant songbirds, as well as residents and nesting species such as prothonotary warblers and Acadian flycatchers.

Glossy Ibis
Photo By: Ed Huberty

whiton's crossing

canoe launch is on the Pocomoke River five miles south of Powellville off Rt. 354. It is about five miles upriver of Porter's Crossing. The river at the bridge site is straight, having been channelized by the CCC in 1930, but the original channel lies just west of the altered version.

As at Porter's Crossing, numerous migrant and nesting songbirds can be seen during spring and fall, and waterfowl can be found in fall and winter. Bald eagles use the area, as do herons and egrets. Prothonotary warblers nest in the wooded swamp.

adkins mill

(Pond) Park is in the town of Powellville on Rt. 354 just north of the intersection with Rt. 350. There is a small parking lot with a covered picnic area by the pond; a small exhibit explains the historic use of the area.

A road leads from the picnic area to a half-mile boardwalk trail into the forest and cypress swamp (although portions of the boardwalk have been somewhat submerged in recent years). Waterfowl and nesting neotropicals, including prothonotary warblers and scarlet tanagers, can be found at the site.

Red-headed Woodpecker

The best times to go are spring and early summer. For more information, call Wicomico County Recreation and Parks at 410-548-4900.

elliott's pond

(a.k.a. West Ocean City Pond) is a good place to see wintering waterfowl, including canvasbacks, redheads, wigeon, (occasionally Eurasian), as well as black-crowned night-herons.

The pond is on Golf Course Rd. off Rt. 50 west of Ocean City. Limited parking is available.

ocean city inlet

can be observed from the beach parking lot at the end of Philadelphia Avenue on the southern tip of the island. In winter, look for purple sandpipers and ruddy turnstones along the rock jetty. The inlet might have eiders, scoters, oldsquaws, harlequin ducks, mergansers, loons, and a variety of gulls. Northern gannets can be seen diving for fish offshore in fall and winter.

Ruby-throated Hummingbird

Black Skimmer
Photo By: Curtis Badger

the 4th street flats

in Ocean City have a variety of birds throughout the year. Waterfowl are common in fall and winter, and royal and common terns nest there in spring and summer. Look for oystercatchers, skimmers, and a variety of shorebirds. The flats are especially productive for shorebirds during migration in spring and late summer.

The flats are on the bay side of Ocean City. From the inlet, follow Baltimore Ave. north, make a left onto 3rd St., and follow that to Sinepuxent Bay, where there are a limited number of parking spaces on the right overlooking the flats.

isle of wight

Wildlife Management Area is at the junction of Rt. 90 and St. Martin's Neck Rd. northwest of Ocean City. A parking area is on the south side of Rt. 90. The upland forest, salt marsh and coastal bay attract migrating and wintering species. Chuck-wills-widows nest here.

For more information, contact the Maryland DNR at 410-543-8223.

great cypress swamp

Delaware Wildlands Conservation Area is at the headwaters of the Pocomoke River near the Maryland-Delaware state line. It's a good place to visit in spring and early summer to see migrating and nesting neotropicals including prothonotary, worm-eating, and hooded (and rarely Swainson's) warblers, plus summer and scarlet tanagers and Acadian flycatchers.

To get to the conservation area, turn north onto Rt. 610 from Rt. 50 at Whaleysville. After 1.3 miles turn left onto Shepard's Crossing Road. Follow this for 3.4 miles until the fork, turn right at the fork onto Nelson Rd. (an unmarked dirt road). After .3 miles, turn right onto Swamp Road (another unmarked dirt road) and park on the side of Swamp Road. Return on foot to Nelson Road, turn right and bird along the road. To return to Rt. 50, continue on Swamp Road 2.3 miles, turn right onto Blueberry Rd, continue on that 3.3 miles to Shepard's Crossing Road, make a left, after .2 miles make a right onto Rt. 610, follow that 1.3 miles until it merges with Rt. 50.

Dunlins
Photo By: Curtis Badger

assateague/chincoteague

Sanderling

What we have here is one large barrier island governed by several different political entities. Since birds rarely observe political boundaries, we will discuss the island in its entirety in a single section.

Assateague is a 37-mile long barrier island reaching from Ocean City Inlet in Maryland to Chincoteague Inlet in Virginia. Chincoteague National Wildlife Refuge is located on the southern (Virginia) portion of the island, while Assateague Island National Seashore occupies most of the Maryland section. Assateague State Park, operated by the Maryland Department of Natural Resources, occupies two miles of the northern end of the island adjacent to the federal property.

In general, the island is good for birding year-round. Freshwater impoundments at Chincoteague NWR hold thousands of waterfowl in fall and winter. Shorebirds can be seen during migration in spring and late summer. The wooded portions of the island are good places to see warblers and other songbirds as they move between nesting areas in the northern U.S. and Canada and wintering grounds in the tropics. Hawks, including peregrine falcons, can be seen during the fall migration, and seabirds can be spotted during the winter months.

assateague island national seashore

To reach the northern (Maryland) end of Assateague Island, take Rt. 50 east toward Ocean City, exiting at Rt. 113 south at Berlin. In Berlin, take Rt. 376 eastward, then turn right onto Rt. 611 and follow it to the

island. The Barrier Island Visitor Center is located on the right just before the bridge, which offers a sweeping view of the northern end of the island, with Ocean City in the distance.

The best way to explore this part of Assateague is by bicycle and by foot. A paved bike path begins near the visitor center, crosses the bridge to the island, and extends southward parallel to Bayberry Drive some four miles to the cul-de-sac where the pavement ends.

Several nice trails branch off the main drive, all of which should be of interest to birders. The national seashore entrance station is about two miles south of the state park parking lot. Just beyond the station, on the right, is a side road worth exploring. Bayside Drive extends less than a mile to a parking area on Sinepuxent Bay. Along the drive a combination of cleared grasslands and shrub thickets creates edge habitat where many birds can be seen. This little finger of land, extending into Sinepuxent Bay, seems to be a magnet for a number of migrating birds.

Snow Goose

Assateague offers three nature trails (hikers only), and the first begins here on Bayside Drive. It is the Life of the Marsh Trail, a loop that extends over and through a salt marsh setting on the edge of the bay. In winter, this is a good place to watch waterfowl feeding in the shallow waters of Sinepuxent Bay.

Other nearby paths include the Life of the Forest Trail and Life of the Dunes Trail, both loops of about a half-mile. The forest trail is especially good for seeing migrating songbirds and resident birds that prefer a forested environment, such as the eastern towhee. If you go, take your binoculars, a bird guide, and insect repellent. If the weather is warm, mosquitoes will be abundant. Migrating warblers will be at peak numbers in April and May and September and October.

Short-billed Dowitcher

American Goldfinch

The dune trail provides a fascinating look at how sand dunes form and how they are sculpted by wind, water, and other forces. The dune environment changes rapidly, and it is possible, upon several visits over a period of time, to document such changes and speculate on how and why they happened. You won't find many songbirds in this open environment, but look for migrating hawks in the fall.

Campsites are available in the state park and in the national seashore.

For information, write to Assateague Island State Park, 7307 Stephen Decatur Highway, Berlin, MD 21811-9741. Phone 410-641-2120.

Assateague Island National Seashore, Rt. 611, 7206 National Seashore Lane, Berlin, MD 21811. Phone 410-641-1441.

chincoteague national wildlife refuge

created in 1943, is one of numerous sanctuaries along the Atlantic flyway the major constituency of which is migratory birds. The impoundments, which were constructed in the early 1950's, are a magnet to snow geese, Canada geese, a wide variety of dabbling ducks, as well as shorebirds.

Chincoteague NWR is reached by taking Rt. 175 from Rt. 13 to the island town of Chincoteague; from there follow the signs to Assateague Island.

Chincoteague NWR is well-known among birders for a number of reasons. Wintering waterfowl are a given, but the maritime forest on the southern portion of the island is a vital feeding and resting area for neotropical migrants, those colorful warblers, tanagers, and related birds that nest in North America and winter in the tropics.

Assateague Lighthouse
Photo By: Curtis Badger

Chincoteague Ponies
Photo By: Ted Deacon

Birding on Assateague
Photo By: Ted Deacon

The shallow ponds and salt marshes that surround the island are home to herons, egrets, bitterns, rails, and other marsh birds. The tidal flats and ponds hold thousands of shorebirds during the peak of migration, and threatened piping plovers nest on the wide beach at the Hook on the southern end of the island and on several other areas.

Birding is good at Chincoteague NWR year-round. Waterfowl begin congregating in October and depending upon the weather, will be on the refuge until spring. April and May are good months to see the neotropical migrant songbirds, and the peak shorebird months are early spring and July and August. September and October mark the busiest days of the fall songbird and hawk migration, with some warblers, notably the yellow-rumped, remaining on the refuge through the winter. There also are large numbers of resident birds, bringing the total that might be seen to more than 300.

A number of trails at the refuge provide access to a variety of habitats. Wildlife Loop, a paved 3.1-mile circuit, begins at the visitor center, which is a short distance from the fee booth. The loop is open to motor vehicles from 3 p.m. until dusk, and the rest of the time access is limited to hikers and bicyclists.

Other trails intersect Wildlife Loop, adding to the miles one may cover as well as the diversity of habitat. The loop runs along the earthen dikes that make up the impoundments and then winds through an upland area and wooded swamp. Black Duck Trail joins the southern portion of the loop and provides hike and bike access to a second paved loop called Woodland Trail, a circuit of about a mile and a half.

Another trail intersects Wildlife Loop, crosses a marsh, and runs behind the dune line to the northernmost parking lot at the beach.

A third option, available only to hikers, is the unpaved service road that branches off the loop and goes nearly to the Maryland line. This is a good place to look for migrating songbirds in spring and fall, and the shallow impoundments along the service road will have many waterfowl in fall and winter. Look for shorebirds here in late summer.

There are no camping facilities on the Virginia portion of the island, but there are plenty on neighboring Chincoteague Island.

For information, write to Chincoteague National Wildlife Refuge, PO Box 62, Chincoteague, VA 23336. 757-336-6122. A National Park Service naturalist is available at the beach in Tom's Cove Visitor Center. Phone 757-336-6577.

map #7
Mid-Shore Virginia and Chincoteague

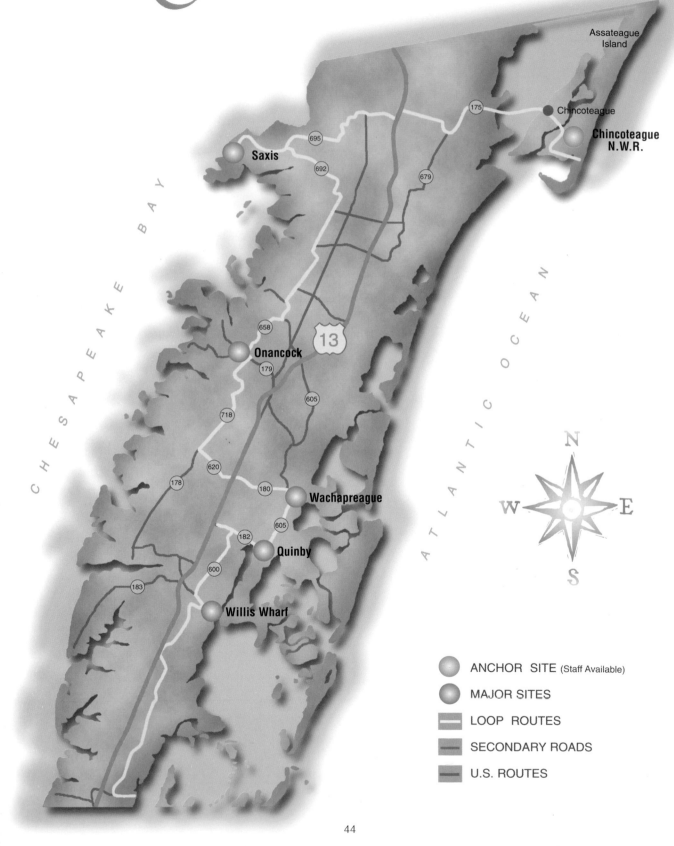

Assateague Island

Chincoteague

Chincoteague N.W.R.

175

695

Saxis

692

679

C H E S A P E A K E   B A Y

658

179

Onancock

13

605

718

620

178

180

Wachapreague

605

182

Quinby

600

183

Willis Wharf

A T L A N T I C   O C E A N

N

W   E

S

ANCHOR SITE (Staff Available)

MAJOR SITES

LOOP ROUTES

SECONDARY ROADS

U.S. ROUTES

the mid-shore from bay to sea

House Wren

The southern tip of Virginia's Eastern Shore and Chincoteague NWR at the northern boundary are the best known birding areas in the Virginia portion of Delmarva, but they are by no means the only birding areas.

Leave U.S. 13 to the tractor trailers and take the back roads, exploring seaside villages, farm fields, and Chesapeake salt marshes. In winter, after a heavy rain, flooded farm fields can hold hundreds of waterfowl and wading birds, so get your scope and go cruising.

the nature conservancy's virginia coast reserve is a sanctuary of more

Cooper's Hawk

than 45,000 acres on 14 barrier islands and the mainland, one of the largest unspoiled stretches of shoreline along the Atlantic seaboard. It represents some of the most important nesting and migratory habitat in the world. It is also a remote, fragile wilderness.

Most of the islands are open to the public for limited day use, but access is by boat only and often difficult. The best way to see the islands is to join one of the Conservancy's educational field trips. All trips are led by a staff naturalist and are scheduled for the peaks of migration in spring and fall. For information, write the Conservancy at Box 158, Nassawadox, VA 23413.

willis wharf

like Oyster, is a seaside village with a colorful history. And like Oyster, it offers excellent birding. Willis Wharf is just off Rt. 600 near the town of Exmore, at the end of Rt. 603 (Willis Wharf Rd.). The road turns south and runs along the commercial waterfront, ending at the marina.

At low tide, extensive mudflats hold shorebirds, including marbled godwits. Whimbrels congregate in the marshes by the thousands in late April and early May, and again in late August. Ruddy turnstones hang around the shucking houses, and diving ducks and wading birds may be seen in Parting Creek. The best time to go is at low tide when the flats are exposed.

Green-winged Teal

Cedar Waxwing

quinby and wachapreague

are just a few miles north of Willis Wharf and are worth a visit for birders. A bridge on Rt. 182 offers a great view of Machipongo River, where waterfowl can be seen in the winter, and wading birds during most seasons. Farm fields can be productive during wet weather, and various raptors can be spotted in the fall.

Wachapreague has a marsh overlook that provides a great view of the seaside salt marshes, Bradford Bay, and Parramore Island in the distance.

onancock

is a bayside town more than 300 years old. It is located at the end of Rt. 179, west of Onley on U.S. 13. Onancock has seasonal ferry service (passengers only) to Tangier Island in the Chesapeake Bay. A few birds can be seen around the wharf area, but a ferry ride will get you out to where the majority of the birds fly. Depending upon the season, you can see brown pelicans, gulls, terns, gannets, petrels, waterfowl, sea turtles, and Atlantic bottlenosed dolphin.

Saxis

is north of Onancock on the Chesapeake and is home to the Commonwealth of Virginia's Saxis Wildlife Management Area. The WMA consists primarily of hundreds of acres of salt marsh, with some upland, mainly hammocks of cedar and pine and saltwater bush. Birding is good in the salt marshes year-round. A number of waterfowl species nest there, as do clapper rail and the elusive black rail. Gulls

Black-crowned Night-Heron

and terns are numerous, and the marshes are home to wading birds such as herons and egrets. Rt. 695 crosses the marsh, providing a good overview. A canoe would be a good craft to explore the marsh further.

Brant

Ring-billed Gulls

The southern tip of Virginia's Eastern Shore

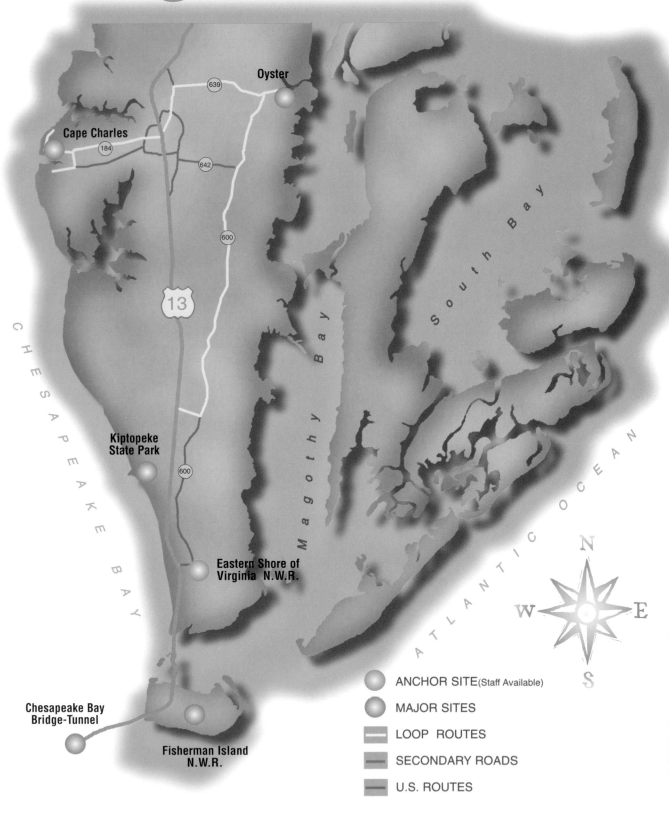

Oyster

639

Cape Charles

184

642

600

13

CHESAPEAKE BAY

Magothy Bay

South Bay

Kiptopeke
State Park

600

Eastern Shore of
Virginia N.W.R.

ATLANTIC OCEAN

Chesapeake Bay
Bridge-Tunnel

Fisherman Island
N.W.R.

N
W E
S

ANCHOR SITE (Staff Available)

MAJOR SITES

LOOP ROUTES

SECONDARY ROADS

U.S. ROUTES

the southern tip

of Virginia's Eastern Shore

Located at the southern point of the Delmarva Peninsula, this narrow strip of land features the unique geology of the confluence of the Chesapeake Bay and Atlantic Ocean to form one of the most important concentrations of birds on the eastern seaboard. A variety of upland habitats, including forests, meadows, farmland and ponds is complemented by miles of unspoiled coastline and acres of saltmarsh, making the area a major Atlantic Flyway resting and feeding stop.

Herring Gulls

This rich diversity of habitats in a relatively small area funnels exceptional numbers of migratory birds including songbirds, falcons and hawks, shorebirds and waterfowl, as well as many nesting species and year-round residents. The local Christmas bird count is one of the highest (150 species) north of Florida.

Fortunately, some of the most fragile and important areas on the southern tip are protected through federal, state, or private conservation ownership. Fisherman Island and Eastern Shore of Virginia National Wildlife Refuges protect the extreme southeast tip. Kiptopeke State Park is on the Chesapeake a few miles north of the refuges. The state also owns Mockhorn Island, a slender, marshy inner island east of the village of Oyster. Smith Island, just north of Fisherman, is protected by The Nature Conservancy in its Virginia Coast Reserve.

Royal Terns
Photo By: Ed Huberty

One of the special birding areas of the southern tip is one of the most unexpected, the Chesapeake Bay Bridge-Tunnel. We'll take a look in this section at all of these public access areas on Virginia's southern tip.

the chesapeake bay bridge-tunnel

spans the 17-mile-wide mouth of the bay as it enters the Atlantic Ocean. From Hampton Roads, it can be reached by taking US Rt. 13 North. From Delmarva, it may be reached by taking US Rt. 13 South. There are four artificial islands on the span, anchoring the ends of the tunnel tubes. The southernmost island, is open to the public. The other three require written permission, which may be gained by writing the CBBT District, PO Box 111, Cape Charles, VA 23310.

The bridge-tunnel islands offer birding otherwise available only by boat. Summer holds a great

Birding from the Chesapeake Bay Bridge-Tunnel
Photo By: Curtis Badger

Hawk Banding
Photo By: Curtis Badger

variety of species, many actively engaged in feeding behavior along tidal rips. Spring and fall migratory seasons can result in many surprises, including birds thrown off their normal migratory paths. In winter, ocean-going birds usually found far off the coast and/or to the north are frequently seen.

Winter features great rafts of waterfowl including all three North American species of scoters, oldsquaws, buffleheads and eiders. Diving flocks of northern gannets are often seen, along with a variety of gulls. Spring and fall migrations include numerous species of shorebirds, songbirds and raptors.

eastern shore of virginia and fisherman island

National Wildlife Refuges are adjacent to the bridge-tunnel property on the southern tip; the bridge crosses Fisherman Island as it exits the Eastern Shore. A visitor center is located on Rt. 600, just off US Rt. 13, with the Eastern Shore of Virginia

NWR entrance a short distance farther east. Fisherman Island NWR is normally closed to the public, but group trips are offered in the fall and winter. Call the refuge at 757-331-2760 for details or ask at the visitor center.

The visitor center is one of the most innovative interpretative facilities in the NWR system and it includes a viewing area overlooking a very productive freshwater pond, where a wide variety of waterfowl can be seen in fall and winter and wading birds during most seasons.

Eastern Shore of Virginia NWR is quite unique when compared to other refuges on the Delmarva Peninsula. You will not see tens of thousands of geese and ducks in large freshwater ponds because this refuge was not established for waterfowl. Millions of neotropical migrants each spring and fall are the featured attraction at this refuge.

The Wise Point raptor banding station on the refuge averages about 800 captures each year. The common raptors that can be seen during that time include American kestrels, sharp-shinned hawks, Cooper's hawks, northern harriers, merlins, ospreys, peregrine falcons and red-tailed hawks. There is also a possibility of seeing red-shouldered, broad-winged and rough-legged hawks as well as bald eagles, golden eagles and northern goshawks.

Another fall visitor that spends time on the refuge is the saw-whet owl. The refuge has one of the three saw-whet owl trapping stations on the southern tip of the peninsula. The Center for Conservation Biology at William and Mary has conducted the trapping program each fall since 1994. Hundreds of saw-whets have been banded by the team.

During the winter, the refuge has a variety of dabbling ducks, wading birds and some of the highest concentrations of American woodcock on the East Coast. On Fisherman Island NWR the sea ducks are often visible during the special tours.

The spring migration is less spectacular than the fall, but is still a great time to birdwatch on the refuge. During a 22-day period between March 15 and May 16, 1998, volunteers from Kiptopeke Environmental Station, Research and Education Laboratory (KESTREL) recorded a total of 49,789 migrant birds of 160 species. There were 13 different species of raptors and 22 different warblers.

The refuge offers a photography blind, nature trails, and viewing platforms that enable you to see a variety of birds "up close and personal". Be sure to climb to the platform atop the old gun emplacement. The view of the bay, ocean, marshes and barrier islands is spectacular, and it is a great place to watch raptors in the fall. The salt marsh overlook yields many wading birds, shorebirds and the clapper rail for those who are patient.

Brown Pelican

kiptopeke state park

is located directly on the Chesapeake Bay. Its sandy beaches, coastal dunes, upland forests, and open meadows provide an array of productive habitat for over 300 species of birds. Since 1963, the banding station has banded over 250,000 birds. The station is manned by volunteers from the Virginia Society of Ornithology and operates from early September until the end of October. Visitors are welcome and many have gotten their first close-up looks at fall warblers here at Kiptopeke. Best time to visit is just after a cold front passes through, stirring the birds along their migratory route.

The Hawk Observatory is open to the public and ranks as one of the top facilities along the Atlantic Flyway. With up to 80,000 raptors counted each fall, and six individual species records, it is a great place to learn about birds of prey. Hawk banding also occurs and programs on these magnificent birds are presented twice weekly. In addition, extensive board-

Peregrine Falcon

Red-breasted Mergansers

Osprey

walks and nature trails provide easy access to habitat for many species of waterfowl, song-birds, gulls and terns, brown pelicans, osprey and wading birds. Atlantic bottlenosed dolphin are often sighted off the beaches.

  The Park offers summer and fall inter-

Northern Harrier
Photo By: Gary Marine

pretive program-ming, camping, a life-guarded beach, fishing pier, boat ramp, a colorful butterfly garden and sheltered picnic areas. KESTREL (Kiptopeke Environmental Station, Research and Education Laboratory) contributes to the under-standing of bird and insect migration and has five major programs at the Park: the Songbird Banding Station; the Hawk Watch; the Raptor Research Station; the Spring Migrant Bird Count; and the Butterfly Garden. KESTREL provides many birding educational services including interpretation for school groups and visitors. The organi-zation is always ready to help visitors.

Great Horned Owl

the village of oyster

is a long-time waterman town, a place, as the name implies, where seafood has been harvested for centuries. In the 19th century,

52

Oyster was the port of embarkation for sportsman heading for the famous hotel on Cobb's Island, which lies about six miles east of town.

To reach Oyster, turn east onto Rt. 646 from US Rt. 13, and proceed to Rt. 600 (Seaside Rd.) and turn left. Seaside Rd. is a Virginia Scenic Byway and offers good birding in its own right. As you drive along, look for kestrels, bluebirds and swallows perched on the phone lines, and ducks, shore birds and waders in low wet areas of farm fields. Go north on Seaside Rd 7.5 miles to Rt. 639 (Sunnyside Rd.) and turn right. Proceed on Rt. 639 for .34 miles to Crumb Hill Road (Rt 1802) and turn left. This leads you to the Oyster boat ramp, good parking and views of the village, its harbor, marshes and mudflats.

Mallards

cape charles

is on the Chesapeake Bay almost due west of Oyster. Rt. 184 from U.S. 13 will take you into the center of town and to the beach and breakwater along the harbor. Cross the railroad bridge on Old Cape Charles Road and turn right onto Bayshore Drive to reach the harbor and the Cape Charles Sustainable Technology Park.

This 200-acre ecological business park contains a network of trails and a natural area preserve overlooking the Chesapeake Bay. It features a half-mile long boardwalk that winds through mixed habitat of meadows and forest

to the shoreline and bay overlook. The Sustainable Technology Park has been enhanced with plantings of native food and shelter species, making the meadows and maritime forest ideal migratory songbird and raptor habitat and it hosts local nesters. Cape Charles' bayfront beach and harbor

Snowy Egret

entrance attract a variety of water birds, as well as concentrations of Atlantic bottlenosed dolphin. The inner harbor shelters wading birds and waterfowl, particularly during winter weather.

The beach and harbor offer nesting osprey, terns, gulls, shorebirds, brown pelicans and wading birds in the spring and summer. Winter can provide views of feeding gannets, gulls, sea ducks, loons, mergansers and grebes. Look for purple sandpipers along the rock jetty.

Ovenbird

American Robin

Delmarva's
tourism information

Delaware

Delaware State Tourism Office
99 Kings Highway
P.O. Box 1401
Dover, DE 19903
302-739-4271
800-441-8846
www.state.de.us

Kent County Tourism
9 East Loockerman Street
Treadway Towers
Dover, DE 19901
800-233-KENT
302-734-1736
www.visitdover.com

Southern Delaware Tourism
P.O. Box 240
Georgetown, DE 19947
800-357-1818
302-856-1818
www.visitdelaware.com

Maryland

Maryland Office of Tourism
217 East Redwood Street
Baltimore, MD 21202
800-MD-IS-FUN

Caroline County Tourism
110 Franklin Street
P.O. Box 149
Denton, MD 21629
410-479-4188

Dorchester County Tourism
2 Rose Hill Place
Cambridge, MD 21613
800-522-TOUR
www.shorenet.net/tourism

Kent County Tourism
100 North Cross Street
Chestertown, MD 21620
410-778-0416
www.kentcounty.com

Ocean City Tourism
4001 Coastal Highway
Ocean City, MD 21842
800-OC-OCEAN
www.ocean-city.com
www.ococean.com

Queen Anne's County
Tourism
425 Piney Narrows Road
Chester, MD 21619
888-400-7787
www.qac.org

Somerset County Tourism
P.O. Box 243
Princess Anne, MD 21853
800-521-9189
skipjack.net/le_shore/visit
somerset

Talbot County Tourism
P.O. Box 1366
Easton, MD 21601
410-822-4606
www.talbotchamber.org

Wicomico County Tourism
P.O. Box 2333
Salisbury, MD 21801
800-332-8687
www.co.wicomico.
md.us/tourism

Worcester County Tourism
105 Pearl Street
Snow Hill, MD 21863
800-852-0335
skipjack.net/le_shore/visit
worcester

Virginia

Virginia State Tourism
901 East Byrd Street
Riverfront West, 19th
Floor
Richmond, VA 23219
800-VISIT-VA
www.virginia.org

Chincoteague Chamber of
Commerce
P.O. Box 258
Chincoteague, VA 23336
757-336-6161

Eastern Shore of Virginia
Tourism
Drawer R
Melfa, VA 23410
757-787-2460

coalition members

DELAWARE
Ashland Nature Center
Bombay Hook National Wildlife Refuge
Delaware Dept. of Natural Resources and Environmental Control
      -Division of Parks and Recreation
      -Division of Fish and Wildlife
Delaware Museum of Natural History
Friends of Bombay Hook Foundation
Prime Hook National Wildlife Refuge
Southern Delaware Tourism Commission

MARYLAND
Assateague Island National Seashore
Blackwater National Wildlife Refuge
Maryland Coastal Bays Program
Maryland Dept.of Natural Resources, Wildlife and Heritage Division
Ocean City Fishing Center
Pickering Creek Environmental Center
Salisbury State University
Salisbury Zoological Park
Ward Museum of Wildfowl Art
Wicomico Convention and Visitors Bureau
Wildfowl Trust of North America, Inc.
Worcester County Tourism Department

VIRGINIA
Chincoteague National Wildlife Refuge
Eastern Shore of Virginia National Wildlife Refuge
Northampton County Sustainable Development Initiative
Kiptopeke Environmental Station, Resource Education Laboratory
Kiptopeke State Park
The Nature Conservancy, Virginia Coast Reserve
Virginia Department of Parks and Recreation
Virginia's Eastern Shore Tourism Commission
Virginia Environmental Endowment

REGIONAL
Delmarva Advisory Council
National Fish and Wildlife Foundation
National Park Service
Rural Development Center, University of Maryland Eastern Shore
U.S. Environmental Protection Agency
U.S. Fish and Wildlife Service

additional funders

Chesapeake Chapter/American Association of Zookeepers
Delaware Tourism Office
Ocean City Fishing Center
Pemberton Historical Park
Somerset County Tourism
Southern Delaware Tourism Commission
U.S. Fish & Wildlife Service Friends Group: Bombay Hook
Virginia's Eastern Shore Tourism Commission
Wicomico County Tourism
Worcester County Tourism

notes